The UNWORRY Doodle Book

Alice James

Designed by
Tilly Kitching

Doodled by
Harry Briggs

With expert advice from
Dr. Angharad Rudkin,
clinical psychologist,
University of Southampton

TIME TO UNWORRY

Everybody worries. It's a completely normal part of life. But you can make it a very SMALL part of your life by taking time every day to relax, de-stress, and work little worries OUT of your system.

This doodling book is a tool to help you UNWORRY. You may find that worries in the back of your mind sort themselves out as you doodle. Doodling can also give worries a place to go, out onto paper through your pencil, so they don't build up and up in your head.

There's no right way to doodle, and there's definitely no wrong way.

Why not treat yourself to some NEW pens or pencils, or sharpen some old pencils to bring them to life.

BUT WHAT IS DOODLING?

Doodling is a little like drawing, except you're not trying to make anything in particular. You're not creating a perfect picture, just gently letting your pen or pencil wander, walk, glide or scratch across the page.

Use the prompts on each page as a starting point and doodle, draw, scribble and sketch your way through the book.

As you doodle, ONLY think about doodling - the feel of the pen in your hand, the look of the wet ink or smooth lead, and the textures and the shades on the page.

Let everything else
float away for a while,
and just DOODLE.

worries float away.

Doodling and writing can give your worries a way out. You get some distance from them and they don't build up in your head.

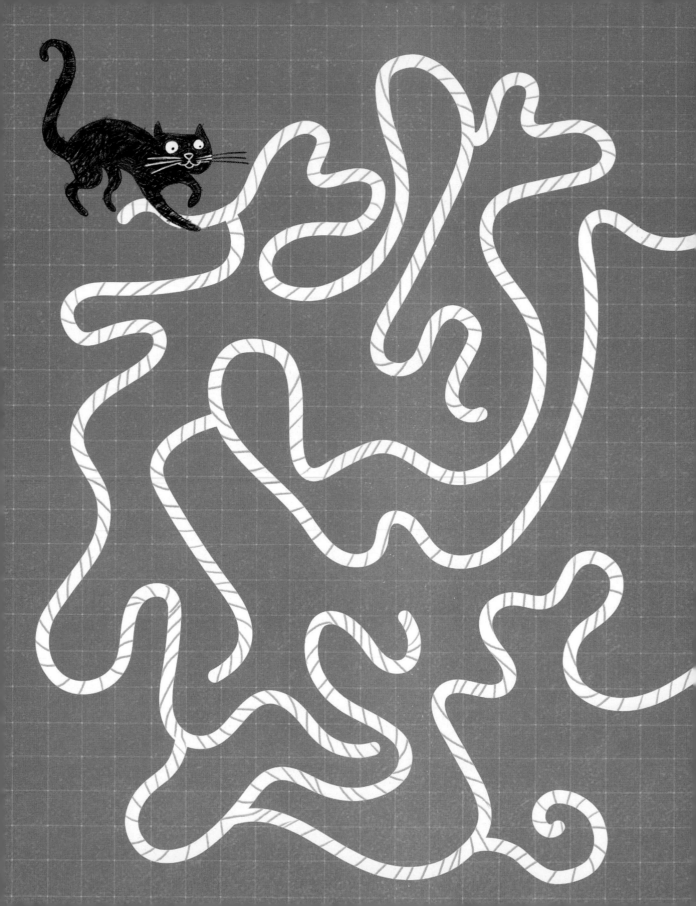

PLINK

You could doodle something particular, or just let your pencil wander across the page.

Getting stuff OUT of your head and onto paper can help to untangle your thoughts.

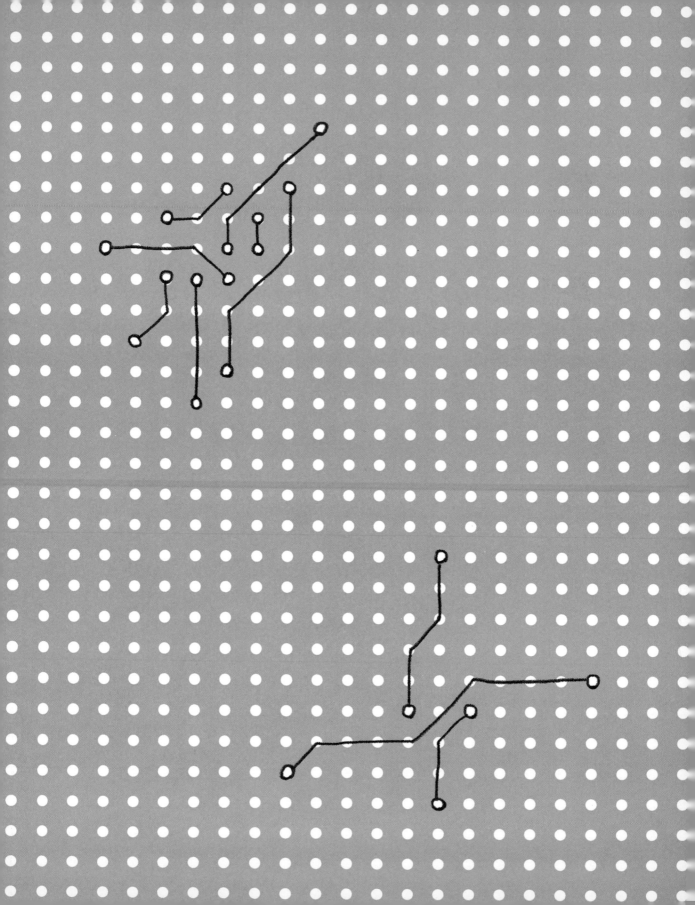

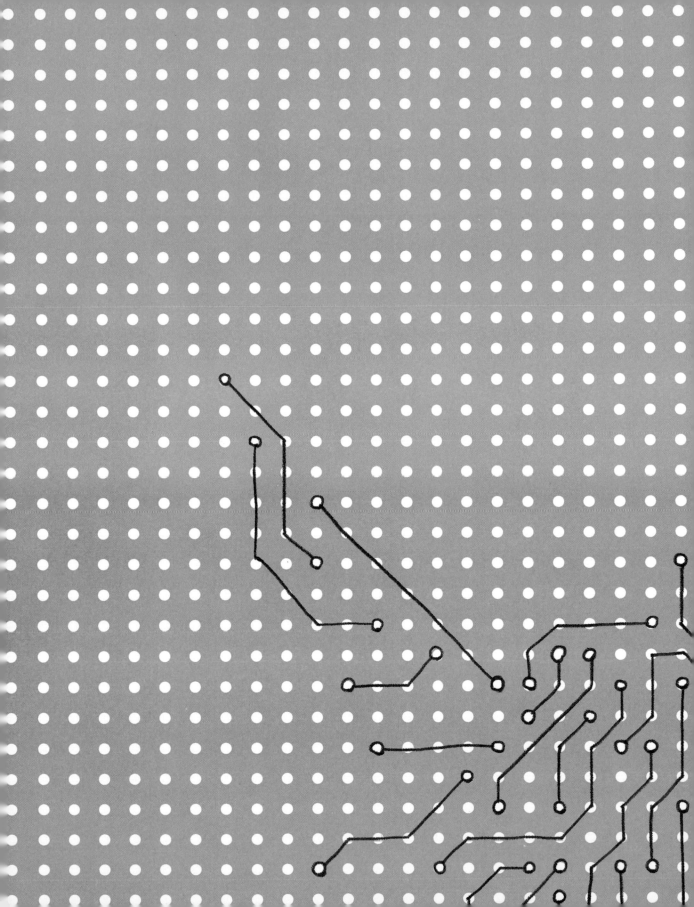

relax Calm

write

unw

doodle

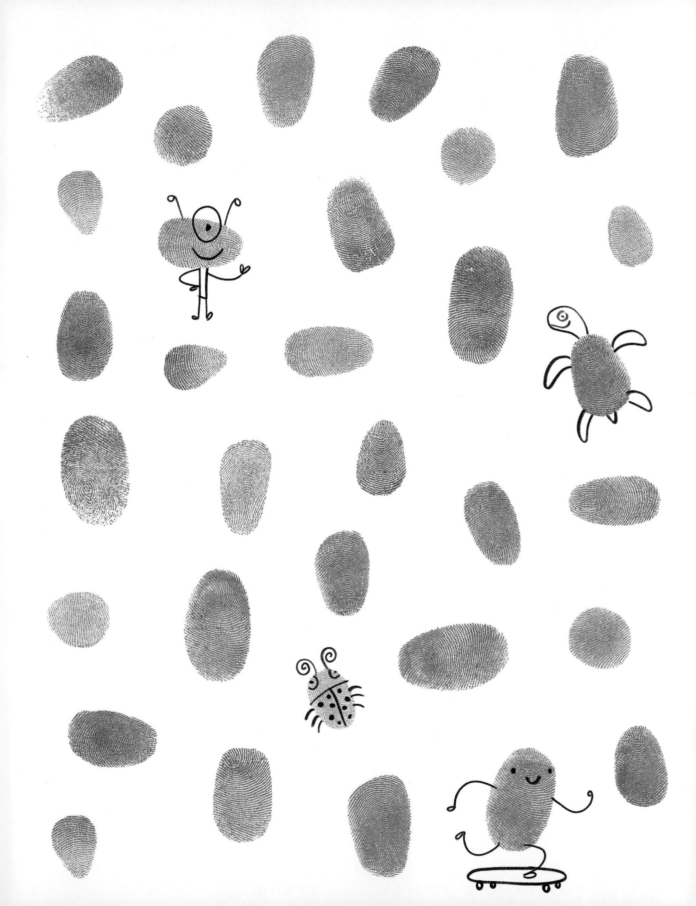

Enjoy a quiet moment to take care of yourself and wrap yourself up in some doodling.

BRRR

ZZZZ

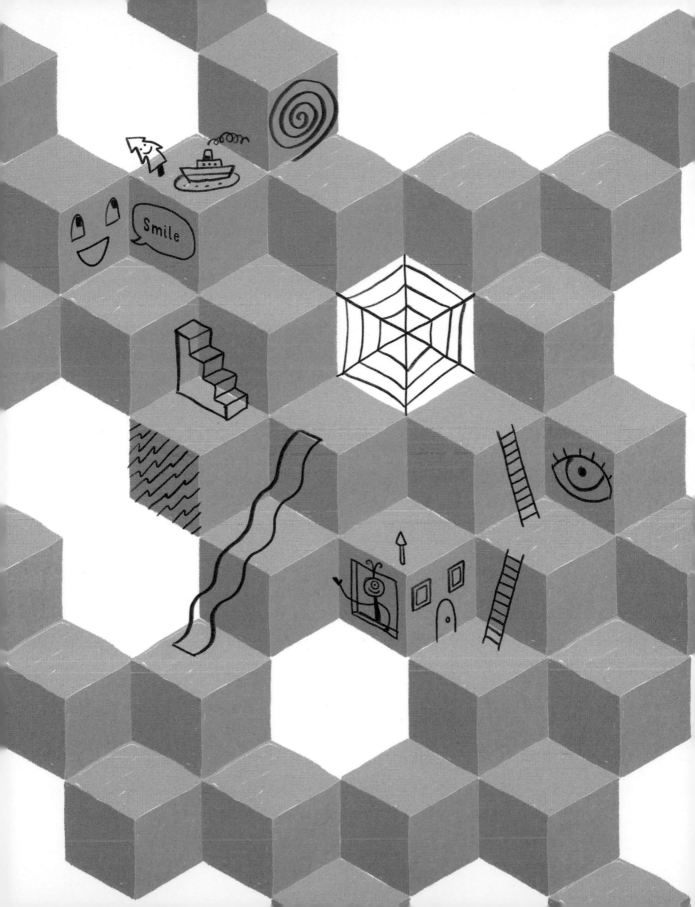

TOOT!

IF YOU'RE STILL WORRIED...

Most of the time, little worries you have will come and go. Taking your mind off things by doing some doodling or another activity, or telling someone what's bothering you is usually enough to make them go away.

If your worries start to take over, and become very loud, it's important to TALK to someone about them. Find a grown-up that you trust, maybe someone at home or at school, and tell them how you're feeling. They will be able to listen and support you, and help you find ways to make the worries more manageable.

Additional illustration by Cristina Martin Recasens

Design manager: Stephen Moncrieff

First published in 2021 by Usborne Publishing Limited, 83-85 Saffron Hill, London EC1N 8RT, United Kingdom. usborne.com